Corner-to-Corner
Lap Throws
for the Family ™

Welcome to the world of corner-to-corner (C2C) crochet. I am so excited to show you this fun and unique way of crocheting! Corner-to-corner crochet blankets are worked just as the name suggests—from corner to corner. By following a pixel graph instead of a written pattern, you can incorporate virtually any character or image you want into a crochet blanket. Add borders or connect smaller squares to create larger blankets. Unlike your typical single crochet graph afghan, the appeal of C2C is speed! These blankets work up much faster than your average project.

Meet designer Sarah Zimmerman: a yarn lover, crafter, blogger, wife and busy mom of three. Sarah is a self-taught crocheter who picked up her first hook shortly after her second child was born. A graduate from the University of Washington with a degree in visual arts and a graphic designer by trade, Sarah has an eye for design and color that is reflected in her crochet projects. Her style can be described as fresh, cute and contemporary designs with a creative flair that appeals to all ages.

Sarah shares her crochet patterns, crafts and slow cooker recipes on her blog Repeat Crafter Me (www.repeatcrafterme.com).

Table of Contents

Getting Started

When working a C2C blanket, you will follow a pixel graph made up of squares. Each row is worked diagonally beginning in the bottom right-hand corner. Each square in the graph represents a beginning chain-3 and additional double crochet stitches.

For the first half of the graph, you will add blocks to each row until you reach the longest diagonal in the graph. After working the longest row, you will begin decreasing. Decreases are made by slip stitching along the last square made.

Basic Instructions

The following sample pattern is a good place to start learning this technique. You will follow the Pattern Graph on page 4 to make a square. The finished swatch is 5½ inches square. You can make several squares and sew them together for a great project!

Pattern Instructions

Row 1

1. Following the Pattern Graph on page 4, ch 6 *(see Photo 1)*, dc in 4th ch from hook. The sk first 3 chs represent the first dc. Dc in each of last 2 chs. You have now completed your first block *(see Photo 2)*.

Row 2

1. Ch 6 *(see Photo 3)*, dc in the 4th ch from the hook and in each of the last 2 chs *(see Photo 4)*. This completes the first block on row 2.

2. Turn *(see Photo 5)*, and sl st in the ch-3 on the first block *(see Photo 6)*. Ch 3 *(see Photo 7)*, work 3 dc in the same ch-3 space. This completes the 2nd block and completes row 2 *(see Photo 8)*.

Row 3

1. Ch 6 *(see Photo 9)*, dc in the 4th ch from the hook and in each of the last 2 chs, turn *(see Photo 10)*.

Photo 9

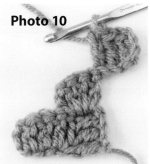

Photo 10

2. Sl st in the ch-3 sp on the next square. Ch 3 and work 3 dc stitches in the same ch-3 space *(see Photo 11)*.

3. Sl st in the ch-3 sp on the next square. Ch 3 and work 3 dc in the same ch-3 sp. You have now completed the 3rd diagonal row *(see Photo 12)*.

Photo 11

Photo 12

Changing Color

Change color when starting a new block by slip stitching with the new color *(see Photos 13a and 13b)*.

Photo 13a

Photo 13b

Using bobbins or small balls of yarn can also be helpful when working with several color changes *(see Photo 14)*. Leave bobbins or small balls of yarn attached until the section is finished.

Photo 14

Do not fasten off old color. Carry the yarn from the previous row when possible *(see Photos 15a and 15b)*.

Photo 15a

Photo 15b

Rows 4–7

Continue working in the pattern, following the Pattern Graph and using the technique you just learned, until you have completed row 7.

Decreasing

When you crochet the last block in the longest diagonal of your chart (Row 7 in the example), you will reach the halfway point of your blanket. Each row after this point will contain one fewer blocks than the row before.

Row 8

1. To begin the next row, sl st in each dc of the last block made on Row 7 and in the ch-3 sp on the same block *(see Photo 16)*. Ch 3 and continue in the pattern to the last block of the row.

Photo 16

2. After working the last block of the row, sl st in the ch-3 sp on the last block of the previous row, turn, and sl st in each dc of the block just worked. Sl st in the ch-3 sp *(see Photo 17)*. Ch 3 and continue in pattern for the next row.

Photo 17

Rows 9–13

Continue working the pattern following the Pattern Graph. At the end of the last row, fasten off.

Tips & Hints

Use the loose ends to your advantage! If you see a color from one block peeking out over another, use the loose ends to weave in over any "mistakes" you want to cover up.

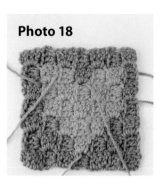

Photo 18

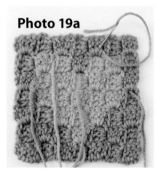

Photo 19a

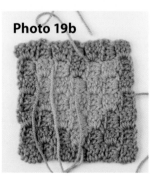

Photo 19b

To help estimate how much yarn you will need, keep in mind that one pixel square is equal to approximately 24 inches of yarn.

Don't let this technique intimidate you. It is very simple once you get the hang of it, and you only need to know a few simple crochet stitches. There is a written pattern provided for you on page 5 to get you started but I'm sure you will quickly find you do not need it!

I hope you have fun with this popular and trendy approach to crochet. I'm sure you will love it as much as I do! ●

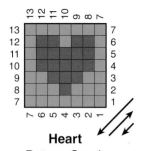

Heart
Pattern Graph
Note: *Arrows indicate direction of work.*

COLOR KEY
■ Perfect pink
■ Tea leaf

Basic Pattern

Skill Level
 EASY

Pattern Notes
Refer to Pattern Graph as needed.

Chain-3 at beginning of row counts as first double crochet unless otherwise stated.

When changing color, carry color not in use on wrong side of piece until needed.

The last increase row is the longest diagonal row on the Pattern Graph.

Pattern

Inc Rows
Row 1: With first color, ch 6, dc in 4th ch from hook *(sk chs count as first dc)*, dc in each of next 2 chs, turn. *(1 block made)*

Row 2: Ch 6, dc in 4th ch from hook and in each of next 2 chs, (sl st, **ch 3**—*see Pattern Notes*, 3 dc) in next ch-3 sp across, turn. *(2 blocks made)*

Row 3: Ch 6, dc in 4th ch from hook and in each of next 2 chs, (sl st, ch 3, 3 dc) in each ch-3 sp across, turn. *(3 blocks made)*

Next rows: Rep row 3, following Pattern Graph for **color changes** *(see Pattern Notes and Stitch Guide)*, until last block of **last inc row** *(see Pattern Notes)* is finished.

Dec Rows
First dec row: Sl st in each dc across to next ch-3 sp, (sl st, ch 3, 3 dc) in each rem ch-3 sp across to last ch-3 sp, sl st in last ch-3 sp, turn.

Next rows: Rep First dec row to last row of Pattern Graph.

Last row: Sl st in each dc across to next ch-3 sp, (sl st, ch 3, 3 dc) in ch-3 sp, sl st in last ch-3 sp.

Leaving long ends for sewing, fasten off all colors at end of last row. ●

Woodland Animals

Skill Level
 EASY

Finished Measurement
40 inches square

Materials
- Red Heart Super Saver medium (worsted) weight acrylic yarn (7 oz/364 yds/198g per skein):

Fox Motif
- 1 skein each #311 white, #505 Aruba sea, #256 carrot and #312 black

Hedgehog Motif
- 1 skein each #320 cornmeal, #365 coffee and #334 buff
- 2 yds #312 black

Owl Motif
- 1 skein each #579 pale plum, #336 warm brown, #360 café latte, #321 gold, #311 white and #312 black

Raccoon Motif
- 1 skein each #311 white, #661 frosty green, #341 light grey and #3950 charcoal

Blanket Border
- 1 skein #311 white
- Size H/8/5mm crochet hook or size needed to obtain gauge
- Tapestry needle

Gauge
1 block = ¾ inch

Pattern Notes
Refer to Getting Started on page 2 as needed.

Refer to Basic Pattern on page 5 as needed.

Yardage is overestimated to allow enough yarn to create multiple working bobbins for color changes.

Border can be made wider by working as many rounds as desired.

Join with slip stitch as indicated unless otherwise stated.

Blanket

Fox Motif
Work pattern as shown in Fox Pattern Graph.

Border
Rnd 1: Join (see Pattern Notes) white in any corner, ch 1, (sc, ch 2, sc) in same corner, sc evenly around Fox Motif, working 2 sc in each ch-3 sp, 3 sc in each dc and (sc, ch 2, sc) in each corner, join in first sc. Fasten off.

Hedgehog Motif
Work pattern as shown in Hedgehog Pattern Graph.

Border
Work same as Fox Motif Border.

Owl Motif
Work pattern as shown in Owl Pattern Graph.

Border
Work same as Fox Motif Border.

Raccoon Motif
Work pattern as shown in Raccoon Pattern Graph.

Border
Work same as Fox Motif Border.

Finishing

Assembly

With RS tog, **whipstitch** (see illustration) along edges of Motifs to join as shown in Assembly Diagram.

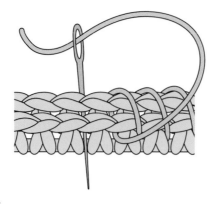

Whipstitch Edges

Woodland Animals
Assembly Diagram

Border

Rnd 1: Join white in any corner, ch 1, (sc, ch 2, sc) in same corner, sc evenly around Blanket, working 2 sc in each ch-3 sp, 3 sc in each dc and (sc, ch 1, sc) in each corner, join in first sc. Fasten off. ●

COLOR KEY
☐ Cornmeal
■ Coffee
▨ Buff
■ Black

COLOR KEY
☐ White
▨ Aruba sea
▨ Carrot
■ Black

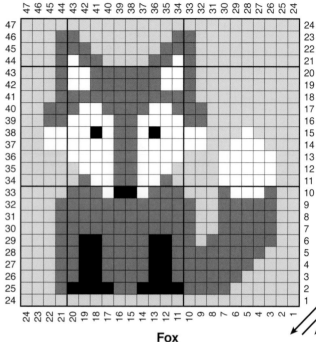

Fox
Pattern Graph
Note: Arrows indicate direction of work.

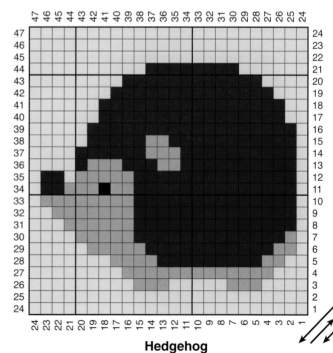

Hedgehog
Pattern Graph
Note: Arrows indicate direction of work.

COLOR KEY

- Pale plum
- Warm brown
- Café latte
- Gold
- White
- Black

Owl
Pattern Graph
Note: Arrows indicate direction of work.

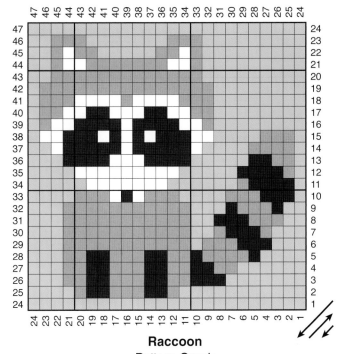

COLOR KEY

- White
- Frosty green
- Light grey
- Charcoal

Raccoon
Pattern Graph
Note: Arrows indicate direction of work.

Simple Stripes

Skill Level

 EASY

Finished Measurement

33 inches square

Gauge

1 block = ¾ inch

Pattern Notes

Refer to Getting Started on page 2 as needed.

Refer to Basic Pattern on page 5 as needed.

Blanket

Work pattern as shown in Pattern Graph. ●

Materials

- Red Heart Super Saver medium (worsted) weight acrylic yarn (7 oz/364 yds/198g per skein): 1 skein each #319 cherry red, #512 turqua, #528 medium purple, #341 light grey, #320 cornmeal, #256 carrot and #311 white
- Size H/8/5mm crochet hook or size needed to obtain gauge
- Tapestry needle

COLOR KEY
- ■ Cherry red
- ▨ Turqua
- ■ Medium purple
- ▨ Light grey
- ▨ Cornmeal
- ■ Carrot
- ☐ White

Simple Stripes
Pattern Graph
Note: *Arrows indicate direction of work.*

Snowman

Skill Level
■■□□ EASY

Finished Measurement
33 inches square

Gauge
1 block = ¾ inch

Pattern Notes
Refer to Getting Started on page 2 as needed.

Refer to Basic Pattern on page 5 as needed.

Choose any color for scarf and earmuffs for a more personal touch.

Join with slip stitch as indicated unless otherwise stated.

Blanket
Work pattern as shown in Pattern Graph.

Border
Rnd 1: Join (see Pattern Notes) turqua in any corner, ch 1, (sc, ch 2, sc) in same corner, sc evenly around entire Blanket, working 2 sc in each ch-3 sp, 3 sc in each dc and (sc, ch 2, sc) in each corner, join in first sc. Fasten off.

Rnd 2: Join white in any ch-2 corner sp, ch 1, (sc, ch-2, sc) in same sp, sc in each sc around, working (sc, ch 2, sc) in each ch-2 sp, join in first sc. Fasten off. ●

Materials

- Red Heart Super Saver medium (worsted) weight acrylic yarn (7 oz/364 yds/198g per skein):
  - 3 skeins #512 turqua
  - 2 skeins #311 white
  - 1 skein each #365 coffee, #256 carrot, #319 cherry red, #624 tea leaf and #312 black
- Size H/8/5mm crochet hook or size needed to obtain gauge
- Tapestry needle

COLOR KEY
- ■ Coffee
- ■ Carrot
- □ White
- ▨ Turqua
- ▨ Tea leaf
- ■ Cherry red
- ■ Black

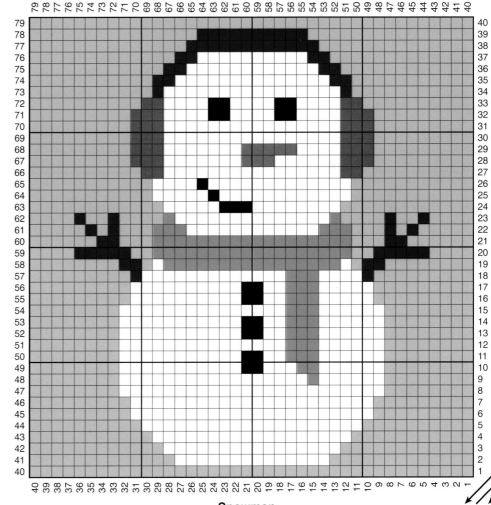

Snowman
Pattern Graph
Note: Arrows indicate direction of work.

Sheep Blanket

Skill Level

 **EASY**

Finished Measurement

27 inches square

Materials

- Red Heart Super Saver medium (worsted) weight acrylic yarn (7 oz/364 yds/198g per skein):
    2 skeins #624 tea leaf
    1 skein each #311 white, #341 light grey and #312 black
- Size H/8/5mm crochet hook or size needed to obtain gauge
- Tapestry needle

Gauge

1 block = ¾ inch

Pattern Notes

Refer to Getting Started on page 2 as needed.

COLOR KEY
- ▨ Tea leaf
- ☐ White
- ▨ Light gray
- ■ Black

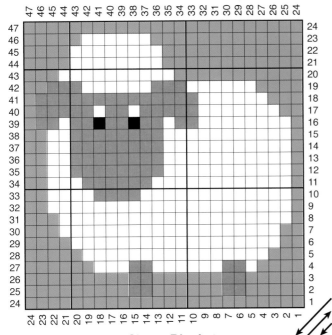

Sheep Blanket
Pattern Graph
Note: Arrows indicate direction of work.

Refer to Basic Pattern on page 5 as needed.

Border can be made wider by working as many rounds as desired.

Join with slip stitch as indicated unless otherwise stated.

Chain-3 at beginning of round counts as first double crochet unless otherwise stated.

Special Stitch

Single crochet join (sc join): Place slip knot on hook, insert hook in indicated st, yo and draw up a lp, yo and draw through both lps on hook.

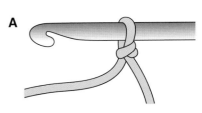
A

B

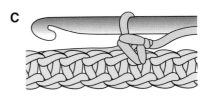
C

Single Crochet Join

Blanket

Work pattern as shown in Pattern Graph.

Border

Rnd 1: Sc join *(see Special Stitch)* white in sp between any 2 blocks, ch 2, [sc in next sp between blocks, ch 2] around, working (sc, ch 3, sc) in each corner, **join** *(see Pattern Notes)* in first sc. Fasten off.

Rnd 2: Join tea leaf in any ch-2 sp, **ch 3** *(see Pattern Notes)*, 2 dc in same sp, ch 1, [3 dc in next ch-2 sp, ch 1] around, working (2 dc, ch 3, 2 dc) in each corner ch-3 sp, join in top of beg ch-3. Fasten off.

Rnd 3: Sc join white in any ch-1 sp, ch 2, [sc in next ch-1 sp, ch 2] around, working (sc, ch 3, sc) in each corner ch-3 sp, join in first sc. Fasten off.

Rnds 4–7: [Rep rnds 2 and 3 alternately] twice. ●

Sweet Dreams

Skill Level

 **EASY**

Finished Measurement

40 inches square

Materials

- Red Heart Super Saver medium (worsted) weight acrylic yarn (7 oz/364 yds/198g per skein):
  3 skeins #381 light blue
  1 skein each #322 pale yellow, #316 soft white, #724 baby pink and #360 café latte
- Size H/8/5mm crochet hook or size needed to obtain gauge
- Tapestry needle

Gauge

1 block = ¾ inch

Pattern Notes

Refer to Getting Started on page 2 as needed.

Refer to Basic Pattern on page 5 as needed.

Join with slip stitch as indicated unless otherwise stated.

Blanket

Work pattern as shown in Pattern Graph on page 18.

Border

Rnd 1: Join *(see Pattern Notes)* blue in any corner, ch 1, (sc, ch 2, sc) in same corner, sc evenly around entire Blanket, working 2 sc in each ch-3 sp, 3 sc in each dc and (sc, ch 2, sc) in each corner, join in first sc.

Rnd 2: Sl st in first ch-2 sp, ch 1, (sc, ch 2, sc) in same sp, sc in each sc around, working (sc, ch 2, sc) in each ch-2 sp, join in first sc. Fasten off. ●

COLOR KEY
- Light blue
- Pale yellow
- Soft white
- Baby pink
- Café latte

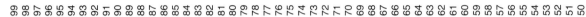

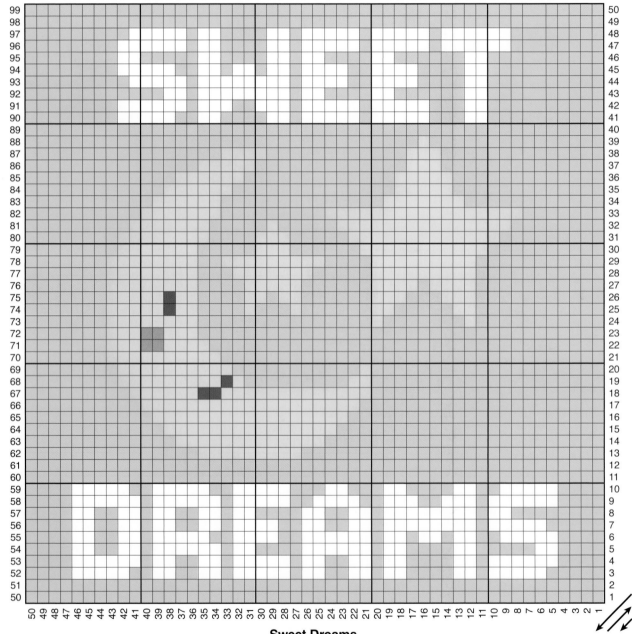

Sweet Dreams
Pattern Graph
Note: *Arrows indicate direction of work.*

STITCH GUIDE

STITCH ABBREVIATIONS

beg	begin/begins/beginning
bpdc	back post double crochet
bpsc	back post single crochet
bptr	back post treble crochet
CC	contrasting color
ch(s)	chain(s)
ch-	refers to chain or space previously made (i.e., ch-1 space)
ch sp(s)	chain space(s)
cl(s)	cluster(s)
cm	centimeter(s)
dc	double crochet (singular/plural)
dc dec	double crochet 2 or more stitches together, as indicated
dec	decrease/decreases/decreasing
dtr	double treble crochet
ext	extended
fpdc	front post double crochet
fpsc	front post single crochet
fptr	front post treble crochet
g	gram(s)
hdc	half double crochet
hdc dec	half double crochet 2 or more stitches together, as indicated
inc	increase/increases/increasing
lp(s)	loop(s)
MC	main color
mm	millimeter(s)
oz	ounce(s)
pc	popcorn(s)
rem	remain/remains/remaining
rep(s)	repeat(s)
rnd(s)	round(s)
RS	right side
sc	single crochet (singular/plural)
sc dec	single crochet 2 or more stitches together, as indicated
sk	skip/skipped/skipping
sl st(s)	slip stitch(es)
sp(s)	space(s)/spaced
st(s)	stitch(es)
tog	together
tr	treble crochet
trtr	triple treble
WS	wrong side
yd(s)	yard(s)
yo	yarn over

YARN CONVERSION

OUNCES TO GRAMS		GRAMS TO OUNCES	
1	28.4	25	⅞
2	56.7	40	1⅔
3	85.0	50	1¾
4	113.4	100	3½

UNITED STATES		UNITED KINGDOM
sl st (slip stitch)	=	sc (single crochet)
sc (single crochet)	=	dc (double crochet)
hdc (half double crochet)	=	htr (half treble crochet)
dc (double crochet)	=	tr (treble crochet)
tr (treble crochet)	=	dtr (double treble crochet)
dtr (double treble crochet)	=	ttr (triple treble crochet)
skip	=	miss

Single crochet decrease (sc dec): (Insert hook, yo, draw lp through) in each of the sts indicated, yo, draw through all lps on hook.

Example of 2-sc dec

Half double crochet decrease (hdc dec): (Yo, insert hook, yo, draw lp through) in each of the sts indicated, yo, draw through all lps on hook.

Example of 2-hdc dec

Reverse single crochet (reverse sc): Ch 1, sk first st, working from left to right, insert hook in next st from front to back, draw up lp on hook, yo and draw through both lps on hook.

Chain (ch): Yo, pull through lp on hook.

Single crochet (sc): Insert hook in st, yo, pull through st, yo, pull through both lps on hook.

Double crochet (dc): Yo, insert hook in st, yo, pull through st, [yo, pull through 2 lps] twice.

Double crochet decrease (dc dec): (Yo, insert hook, yo, draw lp through, yo, draw through 2 lps on hook) in each of the sts indicated, yo, draw through all lps on hook.

Example of 2-dc dec

Front loop (front lp) Back loop (back lp)

Front Loop Back Loop

Front post stitch (fp): Back post stitch (bp): When working post st, insert hook from right to left around post of st on previous row.

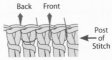

Back   Front

Post of Stitch

Half double crochet (hdc): Yo, insert hook in st, yo, pull through st, yo, pull through all 3 lps on hook.

Double treble crochet (dtr): Yo 3 times, insert hook in st, yo, pull through st, [yo, pull through 2 lps] 4 times.

Treble crochet decrease (tr dec): Holding back last lp of each st, tr in each of the sts indicated, yo, pull through all lps on hook.

Example of 2-tr dec

Slip stitch (sl st): Insert hook in st, pull through both lps on hook.

Chain color change (ch color change) Yo with new color, draw through last lp on hook.

Double crochet color change (dc color change) Drop first color, yo with new color, draw through last 2 lps of st.

Treble crochet (tr): Yo twice, insert hook in st, yo, pull through st, [yo, pull through 2 lps] 3 times.

Metric Conversion Charts

METRIC CONVERSIONS

yards	x	.9144	=	metres (m)
yards	x	91.44	=	centimetres (cm)
inches	x	2.54	=	centimetres (cm)
inches	x	25.40	=	millimetres (mm)
inches	x	.0254	=	metres (m)

centimetres	x	.3937	=	inches
metres	x	1.0936	=	yards

INCHES INTO MILLIMETRES & CENTIMETRES (Rounded off slightly)

inches	mm	cm	inches	cm	inches	cm	inches	cm
1/8	3	0.3	5	12.5	21	53.5	38	96.5
1/4	6	0.6	5 1/2	14	22	56	39	99
3/8	10	1	6	15	23	58.5	40	101.5
1/2	13	1.3	7	18	24	61	41	104
5/8	15	1.5	8	20.5	25	63.5	42	106.5
3/4	20	2	9	23	26	66	43	109
7/8	22	2.2	10	25.5	27	68.5	44	112
1	25	2.5	11	28	28	71	45	114.5
1 1/4	32	3.2	12	30.5	29	73.5	46	117
1 1/2	38	3.8	13	33	30	76	47	119.5
1 3/4	45	4.5	14	35.5	31	79	48	122
2	50	5	15	38	32	81.5	49	124.5
2 1/2	65	6.5	16	40.5	33	84	50	127
3	75	7.5	17	43	34	86.5		
3 1/2	90	9	18	46	35	89		
4	100	10	19	48.5	36	91.5		
4 1/2	115	11.5	20	51	37	94		

KNITTING NEEDLES CONVERSION CHART

Canada/U.S.	0	1	2	3	4	5	6	7	8	9	10	10½	11	13	15
Metric (mm)	2	2¼	2¾	3¼	3½	3¾	4	4½	5	5½	6	6½	8	9	10

CROCHET HOOKS CONVERSION CHART

Canada/U.S.	1/B	2/C	3/D	4/E	5/F	6/G	8/H	9/I	10/J	10½/K	N
Metric (mm)	2.25	2.75	3.25	3.5	3.75	4.25	5	5.5	6	6.5	9.0

Annie's® *Corner-to-Corner Lap Throws for the Family* is published by Annie's, 306 East Parr Road, Berne, IN 46711. Printed in USA. Copyright © 2016, 2020 Annie's. All rights reserved. This publication may not be reproduced in part or in whole without written permission from the publisher.

RETAIL STORES: If you would like to carry this publication or any other Annie's publication, visit AnniesWSL.com.

Every effort has been made to ensure that the instructions in this publication are complete and accurate. We cannot, however, take responsibility for human error, typographical mistakes or variations in individual work. Please visit AnniesCustomerService.com to check for pattern updates.

ISBN: 978-1-59012-787-2
14 15 16 17 18